STUI

FOR INDIVIDUAL AND GROUP USE

RECLAIMING

WHAT IT (REALLY) SAID, WHAT IT MEANS,

VATICAN II

AND HOW IT CALLS US TO RENEW THE CHURCH

FR. BLAKE BRITTON

AVE MARIA PRESS AVE Notre Dame, Indiana

Founded in 1865, Ave Maria Press is a ministry of the United States Province of Holy Cross.

www.avemariapress.com

Paperback: ISBN-13 978-1-64680-228-9

PDF product number: 20124

Cover image © David Lees / The LIFE Images Collection / Getty Images.

Cover and text design by Andy Wagoner.

Printed and bound in the United States of America.

CONTENTS

FOREWORD TO

RECLAIMING VATICAN II

Reclaiming Vatican II could not come at a more opportune moment. Polarization over the Second Vatican Council has reached a new degree of intensity, at least in the public eye. Some prominent prelates of the Church are calling for the rejection of the council altogether, on the grounds that at many points it is at variance with inherited Church teaching, both in letter and in spirit. On the other hand, equally prominent "liberal" interpreters of the council are promoting a wholesale rejection of the letter of the documents in favor of revisionary teaching that represents the true "spirit" of the council, or, what the council *would have taught* if it were not bound by the need to compromise with prominent reactionaries who worked hard to completely block any changes that they perceived to be too "modernist."

These latter "liberals" are styled as "paraconciliar" by Fr. Britton, meaning that the council they "received" and handed on was not Vatican II itself, but a "paracouncil" assembled from the views of dissenting theologians, uninformed and biased media, and from the very cultural tendencies, such as pervasive secularization, which Vatican II was called to address. The paracouncil, in effect, replaced the teaching of the council with its own ideologies. It therefore occluded much of the actual, concrete teaching of the council on matters such as the use of Latin in the Mass, the nature and character of priestly ministry, and its relationship to the royal priesthood of the baptized, the place of Mary in the life of the Church, the way in which the scriptures should be inter-preted, and more. So thoroughly did the ideas of the paracouncil eclipse the ideas of the actual council, that most Catholics came to believe these were the ideas of the actual council. Some, then, in reaction to the paraconciliar ideas that masqueraded as the coun-cil itself, have promoted, in Fr. Britton's language, a "traditional-ist" backlash against the council—or, at least, against what they *think* is the council and its teaching.

In fact, as Fr. Britton so accurately points out, neither camp seems to know the documents themselves very well. The docu-ments seem largely to have been left behind in the heat and fury of competing views. It is not remembered that *Sacrosanctum Con-cilium*, for example, did not call for the wholesale rejection of Latin in the liturgy, but expected that in some ways it would remain normative. Similarly, the calls for inculturation of the liturgy were not intended to displace Gregorian chant or other expressions of the universal Church's one voice. The council did not even man-date celebration of the Mass facing the people. Nor did *Lumen Gentium* use the phrase "people of God" as a new name for the laity, nor did it envision a flattening out of the sacramental, min-isterial priesthood through a quasi-Protestant "leveling" effect relative to the priesthood of all the baptized. Nor did *Lumen Gen-tium* displace Marian devotion by reducing it to an afterthought of ecclesiology or a kind of optional practice to be henceforth rel-egated solely under the category of "popular devotion," meaning it was okay for the uneducated or those from non-Anglo cultures, but otherwise outgrown by the more "enlightened."

My own views on these matters are available elsewhere, so I will not take them up here. Instead, I would like to provide in this foreword a kind of repayment of a debt. A debt of love and gratitude for the council itself, congruent, as I see it, with the sen-timents advanced by Fr. Britton in his call for a recovery and a deeper appreciation of the actual vision of the council.

Fr. Britton points out that the time will soon come when no one is left who will remember being at the council, no one whose life will have encompassed both an experience of the council and an experience of its aftermath. I was too young to be present at the council, but I do remember its earliest implementation, as I was fourteen years old when the council concluded. I was too young to care about, or even know about, Church politics, but not too young to have had a vivid impression of the liturgical reforms as they were phased in. I was absolutely thrilled. My grandmother was not. She repeatedly voiced her distaste, regret, and apprehension at the systematic, though gradual, obsolescence of Latin in favor of English, as well as at the reforms in gesture, manner of celebrating, and so on.

I could not understand her concerns. I do remember realizing, with some dim sense of alarm, that this was a point of no return, and I remember regretting that there would no longer be a universal liturgical language in the Church. But these feelings were overshadowed by the enthusiasm that I felt for finally being able to understand the Mass and to experience it as a living act in which I could participate directly. The Mass had not seemed to be "mine" in any significant way, but rather something that was done, principally, by the specialists in the sanctuary, the priest and the servers. We were not *just* observers, but the sense that we were not just observers was to a large extent dependent on the parts of the Mass that *were* in English and facing the people, namely, the Gospel reading, the homily, and the announcements. The Last Gospel was also in English, and, though it was not read facing the people, I did feel I participated in that weighty moment of utter solemnity and felt a special love for it because I could understand it in all of its poetical gravity.

Couldn't we have followed along in the Missal, in English translation, you might ask? Well, yes—that is, if you could even hear the priest. It was nice that now, due to the reforms, we would be able to *hear* the Mass celebrated. To a varying extent, the prayers of the priest were then often said in a low voice that was inaudible, especially since the words were spoken by someone turned away from the assembly. Also, to read a translation is at the same time to be aware that one is, by that very fact, in some significant sense, "outside" the celebration, which would be otherwise inaccessible.

So many other "markers" seemed to reinforce that feeling of being "outside." Even the sense of reverence and awe associated with the Eucharist could itself be another marker that the Eucharist belonged, essentially, to the priests, whose hands had been specially anointed, as the nuns preparing us for First Communion had told us, while ours had not been. One would no sooner think of picking up a dropped host, should something so unthinkable ever occur, than of painting graffiti on the church walls. Along with the (appropriate) feeling of being unworthy of the Eucharist, there was the additional feeling of somehow being intrinsically impure, ritually impure, which is different entirely. My grandmother, I remember, went to communion only once a year, to do her Easter Duty, at the last possible moment, and she brushed not only her teeth that morning, but her tongue.

The change to English, and to the posture of facing the people, made me feel as though I were accepted and included in this very important and sacred act. I felt as though I belonged, and that it was important that I played my part, and that the liturgy would in some way be lessened (though just as efficacious sacramentally) if I did not. I am a cradle Catholic of the most "standard" variety. I have no dramatic stories of conversion or mystical experiences to report, but simply the dull gratitude for being a member of a Church I am sure I would have not had the courage to join if God had not, in his love, seen fit to bring me into this life in an extended family of practicing believers. I am a member of the lay faithful, ordinary in every way.

Yet I remember one moment of special intensity. For some reason one Sunday I had taken home a monthly "missalette" and during the week began to read the text of the Mass in English from start to finish. I was startled by the beauty of the prayers, by their warmth, their intimacy, and their giving voice to things that seemed to matter to all people. I remember for some reason dwelling especially on the *Agnus Dei* and on the collects. I must have spent a half hour in rapt attention, my heart filling with the warmth of the liturgical words. I felt a true joy and elation at the beautiful words that were prescribed for *me* to say or to listen to attentively. That feeling has never left me. It was the closest thing to an interior "conversion" that I can recall. Even when I am in a foreign country and the liturgy is in a language I do not know, I still "understand" it because I can say it to myself in English, these beautiful things, these same sentiments full of nobility, dignity, and gratitude.

Later on, as a sophomore at a very secular liberal arts college, I remember, almost in desperation for something less cynical and more idealistic than anything on offer in many of the texts read in my classes, picking up a copy of the documents of Vatican II. I opened them at random and lit upon *Gaudium et Spes.* Although it was a seeming waste of time, because I got no course credit for it and certainly no recognition, I could not put the text down. I just kept reading and could not get enough. The questions raised were *my* questions, and the *Church* was interested in them! My soul was lit on fire with the Church's confidence that she had the answers to these questions and could offer a repository of wisdom that rose above the relativism of the so-called learned discourse that denied human dignity or could express it only in one-dimensional, Marxist terms. Going on to *Lumen Gentium*, my heart was indelibly marked, I felt, by the sublimity of the teaching of the "universal call to holiness." I wanted to live up to that. I felt fixed in that ideal. Reading chapter 5 of *Lumen Gentium* ignited a kind of zeal in me and even today I still feel it, and I reread that chapter with ever-new gratitude, every time I have occasion to teach this text.

Reading these documents was motivation enough for me to start going to daily Mass, to visit the Blessed Sacrament in between times, and also to picket the local A&P on Saturday mornings in solidarity with the United Farmworkers Union. I also came to decide that, although I did not feel a vocation to the priesthood, I could contribute to evangelization through the "return to the sources" and the recovery of their teaching in a way attuned to modern questions, as a theologian. My heart was on fire to do so, and, to tell the truth, it still is. That is the debt of gratitude and love that I owe to Vatican II: my whole life as an adult Catholic.

Turning back to the categories of reception that Fr. Britton lays out: With regard to the "traditionalists," I think many of them—especially the younger of them, many of whom belong to the professional, educated social sectors—underestimate how much they owe to the very council they sometimes seem to want to disown. The sense that the Tridentine Latin liturgy is more aesthetic and more reverent is partly a function of the reforms of Vatican II that moved away from a culture that routinely permitted twenty-minute Masses hastily said *soto voce* and without a homily. Furthermore, these beautiful younger people experience the Tridentine Mass with Vatican II sensibilities that they simply take for granted, namely, that they are included as an important constituent of the celebration of the Mass, and are not just, in effect, second-class participants observing from the perspective of the vaguely ritually impure spectator.

On the other hand, as for the paracouncil, the more I was drawn into the documents of Vatican II, especially as I began to use them to teach, the more I was struck by the "silence" that seemed imposed on the documents, selectively, in public discourse and theological literature. For example, the *Catechism of the Catholic Church* was critiqued upon its publication for not having a sufficiently critically informed sense of scripture in accordance with *Dei Verbum*, while the *Catechism*'s extensive use of the "analogy of faith" and the sense of scripture as a whole precisely as called for by *Dei Verbum* was left without comment, in silence. In fact, the *Catechism* uses scripture in exactly the same way as the documents of Vatican II themselves. Particularly jarring was the way in which, as Fr. Britton notes, the council called for the continuing relevance of Latin as a liturgical language, when in fact it came to be a mark of one's liturgical backwardness to even suggest that Latin should have some kind of continued presence in the public prayer of the Church. The Church in the United States seems to lack imagination in comparison with many of the

African churches that manage to combine Latin and the vernacular in ways that display a connection to the most ancient traditions—in contrast to the Pentecostal churches that compete for the allegiance of Catholics—while setting them in the context of an authentic African sensibility.

Overall, however, I have had the faith, and continue to have the faith that, as Fr. Britton suggests, the documents of Vatican II—spirit, content, and all—can still today provide the inspiration for meaningful reform in the Church and for the evangelization of the "modern world." This work will not be accomplished in the glare of publicity, as though media attention were what made it important, but rather without fanfare, in the implementation, little by little, of the vision of the council in the ordinary life of the parish. This will mean the patient cultivation of a liturgical sensibility of awe, and yes, unworthiness, at the lavishly loving sacrifice of the Lord, accomplished on the Cross and still poured out for us even today in the Eucharist. This is not primarily the awe of an aesthetic, but the awe at a mystery of love of which indeed we are not worthy and therefore for which we learn to be more and more grateful. Let this awe spill over into the related awe at the dignity of the human person and of the beauty of the world that "God so loved" that sacrifice of Christ's Precious Blood was not unthinkable. The works of love and mercy in response—for example, the work of parenting and of caring for the poor and for those in need of comfort—are also not glamorous. They are often hidden and seemingly inefficient. Yet all of this provides the ingredients of a renewal of culture based in faith, truth, and beauty, that can truly be, over time, a persuasive response to the "joys and hopes, the griefs and anxieties" of our own world, at the same time so precious and so troubled.

John C. Cavadini

INTRODUCTION

Since its publication, *Reclaiming Vatican II* has been reviewed in numerous circles among Catholic, Protestant, and secular outlets. Furthermore, in addition to the average reader, we have received letters from bishops, seminary faculty, chancery offices, theologians, and historians around the world expressing their support and gratitude, while offering insights to their local experience of the Church. Even more edifying is the number of requests to provide study materials for the text so that parishioners and individuals alike might come to a better understanding of Vatican II and its true mission. It was the frequent request for such materials that has led to the publication of this study guide. In addition to overwhelming the author with a spirit of thanksgiving, these communications have revealed the real-world consequences of the book and how it is affecting people's lives.

After reading thousands of messages, two reoccurring themes emerged. Firstly, many people were not aware of the distinction between the council and the paracouncil. They knew something wasn't quite right about the general reception and implementation of Vatican II, but they couldn't name it nor explain its origins. Learning about the paracouncil and its influence on the so-called "Spirit of Vatican II" was an epiphany that helped them distinguish between popular narratives about the council and the true intention of the council per se.

The second theme was an appreciation of the overall tone of the book and its way of addressing different topics, especially certain sensitive subjects such as the liturgy and traditionalism. Rather than striking the usual tone of defensiveness or aggression so commonplace in the realm of social media, *Reclaiming Vatican II* discussed flashpoints of controversy with an air of freedom, respect and objectivity recognizing that every Christian, no matter where they fall on the religious spectrum, is still trying to love Christ and the Church. This appreciation for the attitude of the text betrays an underlying exhaustion prevalent in our society with the inability to dialogue civilly and respectfully. The moment we turn on the news, we are hammered with polemics and theater. It is difficult to find integrity and a genuine desire to communicate. It is refreshing to see someone sincerely trying to make a point while honoring the other perspective.

These observations reinforced by thousands of readers show that *Reclaiming Vatican II* is starting a different kind of conversation about the council, one which many people did not even realize needed to happen, namely, the distinction between Vatican II, paraconciliarism, and traditionalism. Nowadays, many commentators approach the council from opposite sides of the spectrum: Either (1) they applaud the council *carte-blanche* invoking its name when convenient to support certain initiatives and programs, but without catechizing on its foundational teachings, or (2) they renounce it as a new-age phenomenon that has splintered the Church and needs to be wholly revoked. Neither of these perspectives hold water.

The tension between these two camps—inappropriately labeled "liberal" and "conservative" Catholicism—has disproportionately influenced the last fifty years of theological conversation and liturgical praxis. As a result, the council remains a hotbed of discrepancy for certain members of the Church while the vast majority of Catholics in the pew remain indifferent about Vatican II. However, there is another way to understand the council, one that is not bound to polarizing tensions. That was the purpose of *Reclaiming Vatican II* from the get-go. To lay aside the past decades of conflict and pick up the teachings of the council with a humble heart seeking only God's will by trusting the Church.

That leads to one last point about the overall response to *Reclaiming Vatican II*, namely, it reveals that there are tens-of-thousands of Christians willing and able to embrace the council anew.

This is especially true among Millennials and Zoomers (also known as Gen Z). It is surprising and inspiring to see the number of young Catholics who are reading the book. Unlike their predecessors, they did not live during the time of the council nor did they experience the immediate implementation phase. They approach Vatican II topics typically deemed "controversial" by Boomers and Gen X (for example, Latin, *ad orientem*, sexuality and marriage, social justice, and so on) with a kind of sincerity that is uninfluenced by agendas and unrestricted by baggage. Younger generations discuss these issues much more freely and review Church tradition without the anxiety of being "pre–Vatican II" or "post–Vatican II." Those terms are meaningless to Millennials and Zoomers. Confronted, as we are everyday by the obstinacy of secularism, our main concern is the essential nature of the Church and the foundational principles of Christianity. Likewise, we are open to expressing the faith in whatever modes are most effective whether they be from the sixteenth century or the twenty-first makes little difference. Truth is timeless, and some things just work no matter what year they are utilized. In that regard, an increasing number of younger Catholics are beginning to read and study Vatican II with fascination, finding in the documents a bedrock on which to launch a new age of missionary discipleship rooted in tradition and evangelization.

As we provide this study guide for *Reclaiming Vatican II*, it is done with great hope for the future of the Church. The enthusiasm with which our readers have endorsed the book is both touching and inspirational. We want to thank the many readers and supporters who have helped bring this most recent project to fruition. Your feedback and counsel have proved invaluable.

As readers work through *Reclaiming Vatican II* and this study guide, they may find that they would like to take notes on what they've learned, whether through study or reflection. We have provided pages in the back of this guide for that very purpose. We encourage the reader to discern ways in which the Lord is calling them to fulfill the vision of the Council in their own lives.

We pray that this study guide will build on the momentum of renewed vigor for a deeper knowledge of the council documents so that we might be the generation who works to reclaim Vatican II to the glory of God and the salvation of souls. Praised be Jesus Christ, now and forever!

Your servant and priest in Christ,

Fr. Blake Britton

CHAPTER 1

THE PARACOUNCIL: WHAT HAPPENED?

Chapter Summary

Vatican II is a point of contention for many within the Church. Tensions permeate social media and other places of discourse with so-called "traditional" and "liberal" Catholics disagreeing about Vatican II's supposed implications. But both sides are laboring under some serious misunderstandings. As outlined in the introduction of *Reclaiming Vatican II*, both liberal and traditional camps are responding to what Henri de Lubac calls "the para-Council"—a poor caricature of what the council really taught. Thus, before we can reintroduce ourselves to Vatican II's true spirit and begin to reclaim its legacy for the Church, we need to get a better handle on what led to its misimplementation in the first place. There are three main sources for the paracouncil: 1) The council of the theologians, 2) the council of the media, and 3) the council of the age.

The council of the theologians refers to certain theologians who, instead of adhering to the documents of the council as written decided to follow what they called "the spirit of Vatican II." In setting aside the texts and focusing instead on the council's "spirit," a vast margin was left open for the question on how this spirit was to be implemented. In lieu of promoting the documents as written and in cooperation with the magisterium, certain theologians presented the teaching of the council through the lens of their own theological agenda, foisting themselves on public opinion as authentic interpreters of the council.

The council of the media refers to media outlets becoming a mouthpiece for theologians promoting their personal interpretations of the council as well as the media's parceling of the Church into liberal and conservative factions. It is inappropriate to interpret the Church through political categories. The Church intersects constantly with our social and political realities, but we must remember that the Church is a divine institution that must be understood in a spiritual way. To interpret Church actions as nothing more than a skirmish between liberal and conservative groups will always prove insufficient and lopsided. Yet that is exactly what the media did when reporting on Vatican II. The effects of this kind of thinking is still negatively influencing dialogue in the Church.

The council of the age refers to the cultural and historical context that shaped the overall reception of the paracouncil and Vatican II. The 1960s and 1970s were a turbulent time in world history. In an age when doing unconventional things was heroic and casting off the shackles of antiquity was a virtue, certain theologians' interpretations of the Second Vatican Council appeared to be yet another way of "sticking it to the man." For some in the Church, Vatican II signaled that Catholicism was ready to sync-up with the society's revolutions and ideologies. This likewise usurped the overall message of the council.

Not everyone received the paracouncil with enthusiasm. In the decades following Vatican II, clergy and laity alike sought a return to tradition as a means of coping with the changes spreading throughout the Church under the paracouncil's influence. However, many of the issues raised by traditionalist groups, especially in regard to the liturgy, are not contentions with the council itself but rather with the ways in which specific individuals promoted paraconciliar opinions. Reclaiming Vatican II will be key in uniting these opposing trends in the Church and moving forward as one Body in Christ.

Chapter Outline

I. The current understanding of Vatican II in the Church

   A. Decades after its closing session, Vatican II continues to be a point of contention for many Catholics

      i. This has led to the development of two camps in the Church each with their own interpretation of Vatican II

         1. Paraconciliarists, also known as "liberal" Catholics

         2. Traditionalists, also known as "conservative" Catholics

      ii. How did these opposing views of the council form?

II. The origins of the paracouncil

   A. What is the paracouncil?

      i. An interpretation of the Second Vatican Council's teachings rooted in personal ideologies or political and theological agendas that contradict the officially promulgated texts and intentions of the council itself

   B. Three major sources of the paracouncil

      i. The council of the theologians

         1. A term used to describe the post-conciliar theologians who are dismissive or disappointed in the declarations of the council and utilize the implementation phase (1965–present) as an opportunity to promote their personal theologies while claiming to act in the so-called "Spirit of Vatican II"

      ii. The council of the media

1. A term used to describe the mass media's misrepresentation of Vatican II as a political event. It is due to the influence of media outlets that the labels "conservative" and "liberal" are now mainstream in Catholicism. Fr. Blake calls this the "liberal-versus-conservative narrative." The introduction of a political and polarizing commentary into Catholic culture continues to have negative consequences as people now place themselves into ideological camps as opposed to seeing the Church in dialogue

   iii. The council of the age

1. A term used to describe the overarching cultural, political, economic, and religious movements present in the immediate implementation phase of Vatican II (1965–1980). This ambience greatly influenced the general reception of the council and the paracouncil

C. Fall-out from the paracouncil

   i. These three influences (that is, the council of the theologians, the council of the media, and the council of the age) led to a largescale misimplementation of the Second Vatican Council on multiple levels. Several generations of Catholics were misinformed about the true purpose of Vatican II, leading to a variety of practices and abuses—liturgical or otherwise—that did not represent the authentic vision of the council. Furthermore, many of the graces intended by the council have yet to be realized or shared with the People of God

III. The origins of traditionalism

A. Conservative reaction to the paracouncil

   i. As a response to the disingenuous presentation of Vatican II by the paracouncil and the resulting issues, a number of clergy, religious, and laity rebelled against the council and sought to negate its seemingly disastrous effects. This is especially true in regard to the sacred liturgy

ii. This reaction is known as the "traditionalist" or "conservative" movement due to their desire to return to the traditional practice of Catholicism before the reforms of Vatican II

1. The most prominent of these groups is the Society of St. Pius X (SSPX) founded by Archbishop Marcel Lefebvre although there are several others

iii. The majority of criticism hurled against Vatican II by traditionalists is unfounded. In fact, they are reacting to the paracouncil, *not* the Second Vatican Council

1. Traditionalists claim Vatican II got rid of Latin in the Mass when in fact it did the opposite. The council reasserts the indispensable role of Latin in Catholic tradition and the need to retain it in the liturgy (that is, *SC* 50–60)

B. A path forward for the paracouncil and traditionalism

i. Fr. Blake holds that the way to reconcile with traditionalists disenfranchised with the Church is by reclaiming the original intention of Vatican II. Likewise, there needs to be pastoral initiatives to educate the faithful on the documents themselves as opposed to other people's interpretations of the texts. This will safeguard against any false narratives that may be peddled in the name of Vatican II as well as help in defending the council's legitimate purpose

Study Questions

1. What is the paracouncil and what are its three major sources?

2. Describe briefly in your own words the council of the theologians, the council of the media, and the council of the age.

3. Can you name any particular consequences of the paracouncil? Any you have personally been affected by or witnessed?

4. Explain the origins of the modern traditionalist movement and some of their criticisms against Vatican II.

Key Terms

The paracouncil (pp. 1–2)

The council of the theologians (pp. 2–6)

The council of the media (pp. 6–10)

The council of the age (pp. 10–11)

Traditionalism (pp. 11–14)

Society of St. Pius X/SSPX (pp. 11–12)

Archbishop Marcel Lefebvre (p. 11)

CHAPTER 2

THE TRUE SPIRIT OF VATICAN II

Chapter Summary

A period of tension and confusion following an ecumenical council is nothing new in Church history. There are multiple examples, especially among the Church Fathers, of turmoil disseminating among the faithful in the immediacy of a post-conciliar period. One of the best examples comes from St. Vincent of Lerins and his considerations after the Council of Ephesus. St. Vincent's book, *Commonitory*, was dedicated to explaining the development of Christian dogma while providing guidelines for the proper interpretation of conciliar teachings. His description of upheaval after the Council of Ephesus is eerily familiar to our own time. On the one hand, St. Vincent identifies a group of theologians who were seeking adulterated novelty in Church doctrine by casting off antiquity and promoting personal interpretations of the Catholic faith. On the other hand, he mentions those who were unopen to reform and denied the legitimacy of the council.

As St. Vincent points out, the Church is both conservative and progressive insofar as she seeks to conserve the objective truths of her tradition while constantly finding new ways to relate those truths to the world. The two terms used to describe this tradition and progression in regard to Vatican II is *ressourcement* and *aggiornamento*.

Ressourcement (literally, "a return to the sources"), refers to the council's intention to integrate sacred scripture and the theology of the ancient Church Fathers into the common life of the faithful. In regard to the study of sacred scripture, numerous advancements have been made since the Council of Trent (1545–1563). These advances were prompted by a series of landmark discoveries in the eighteenth, nineteenth, and twentieth centuries. Many of the theological points made during the council, especially in regard to ecclesiology, scripture, liturgy, and Mariology were informed by the accomplishments of the *Ressourcement* movement.

Aggiornamento is an Italian word that means "bring up to date." It was popularized by St. John XXIII, who used the word in a speech he offered on the Feast of the Conversion of St. Paul, January 25, 1959, at the Basilica of St. Paul Outside the Walls in Rome. *Aggiornamento* is not a mere progressivist ideology or anti-traditionalism. It is not simply calling for the Church to be modernized or to "get hip with the times." It is much deeper than that. St. John XXIII is inviting the People of God to follow St. Paul's example and awaken a passion for preaching the Gospel through a renewed encounter with the tradition of the Church. *Aggiornamento* therefore presupposes *ressourcement*.

Vatican II represents a major pivot in evangelical and theological style; it is reflective of the style found in the ancient commentaries and writings of the Church Fathers. The conciliar documents read like spiritual works. The ordering of the documents also shows the "logic of Vatican II." They begin with the sacred liturgy (*Sacrosanctum Concilium*), for it is the liturgy that nourishes and sustains the Church. The liturgy is her central activity and most important responsibility, the wellspring from which the Church's identity flows (*Lumen Gentium*). The Church is directed by the grace of divine revelation (*Dei Verbum*), as shown forth through sacred tradition and sacred scripture. Finally, under the guiding hands of divine revelation she is able to evangelize the modern world (*Gaudium et Spes*).

Chapter Outline

I.   Understanding development in Church teaching

   A.   Every council of the Church is followed by a period of confusion, tension and disagreement as people seek to implement and interpret the magisterium's teachings

      i.   There are multiple examples of this fact throughout Church history

         1.   St. Vincent of Lerins and the Council of Ephesus (ca. AD 431)

            a.   In his book, the *Commonitory*, Vincent addresses the conflict between two opposing groups among the hierarchy and laity who either misunderstood or rejected the council's teachings

            b.   St. Vincent denotes the essential relationship between *tradition* and *renewal*

         2.   In regard to Vatican II, these terms are described as *ressourcement* (tradition) and *aggiornamento* (renewal)

II. *Ressourcement* and *aggiornamento*

   A.   *Ressourcement*

      i.   French word literally meaning "a return to the sources"

         1.   Used to describe a period of theology from the eighteenth to the twentieth centuries in which apostolic, biblical, liturgical, and patristic resources are discovered and made widely available to the universal Church

         2.   One of the main catalysts for the Second Vatican Council

      ii. Led to a resurgence of philosophical and theological study in contradistinction to neo-Thomism

      1. Specifically attributed to the fields of liturgy, ecclesiology, Mariology, pneumatology, and biblical theology

        a. Johann Mohler, Henry Newman, Matthias Scheeben, and so on

    iii. A proper understanding of *ressourcement* provides a healthy alternative to traditionalism while still maintaining the integrity of tradition

B. *Aggiornamento*

    i. Coined by St. John XXIII

      1. An Italian word summarized as "renewal" or "freshness"

        a. Often misinterpreted as a rejection of tradition, but in fact is a reaffirmation of the importance of tradition and the need to actively engage tradition in the daily life of the Church

          i. Analogy of the water well

          ii. *Aggiornamento* and *ressourcement* meant to work in tandem not opposition

III. The style and logic of Vatican II

A. Kerygmatic and patristic in character

    i. *Baltimore Catechism* versus the *Catechism of the Catholic Church*

B. Logic of Vatican II

    i. The Second Vatican Council possesses an inherent logic built on the ordering of its documents

      1. Sacred liturgy

      2. The Church

      3. Divine revelation

      4. The Church and the modern world (evangelization)

Study Questions

1. Who was the fifth-century saint who helped to clarify the understanding of development and progress in Church history?

2. What two words describe the source of Vatican II and its mission?

3. Define and describe *ressourcement.*

4. Define and describe *aggiornamento.*

5. What is the logic behind the ordering of the Vatican II documents?

Key Terms

St. Vincent of Lerins (pp. 19–20)

Ressourcement (pp. 21–29)

Aggiornamento (pp. 29–32)

Logic of Vatican II (p. 35)

CHAPTER 3

THE SACRED LITURGY

Chapter Summary

It's no coincidence that the first document published by the Second Vatican Council was *Sacrosanctum Concilium*. The primacy of this document is a deep spiritual truth about the place of worship in Christian living, namely, that adoring and glorifying God comes before all else. We encounter God most intimately in and through worship. The liturgy is not just one activity among many. Rather, it is "a sacred action surpassing all others. No other action of the Church can equal its efficacy by the same title and to the same degree" (*SC* 11).

Of all the topics from Vatican II, none is more controversial in our own time than the liturgy. This is ironic considering that it was the least controversial document at the council itself, being promulgated in 1963 by over 95 percent of the voting bishops. There are two popular responses to the council's reforms. On the one hand, there is an inclination to focus on the council's pastoral component while overlooking its theological and spiritual foundations. On the other hand, those who regard Vatican II with suspicion generally accept the notion that the council desecrated the liturgy. This is usually based on negative experiences Catholics suffered as a result of paraconciliar ideologies in the years immediately following the council.

The Second Vatican Council describes Christ's mission and the basis of the sacred liturgy in two ways: *the redemption of mankind* and *the perfect glorification of God*. We could summarize these points with the words "reconciliation" and "adoration." St. Paul reminds us of the connection between Adam's failure and Christ's triumph as a "ministry of reconciliation" (2 Cor 5:18). Jesus is the one who comes to restore humanity's original intimacy with the Father; he brings us "eyelash-to-eyelash" with God. Likewise, Jesus becomes man to restore right worship of the Father. Put simply, Jesus comes to adore the Father. The word "adoration" comes from the Latin *ad-ora*, literally "mouth-to-mouth." Adoration presupposes reconciliation and is its natural consequence. The liturgy, therefore, is the continued reconciliation and adoration of Christ realized through the sacramental life of the Church.

A guiding principle of Conciliar reform was active participation. Unfortunately, the council's notion of active participation was all too easily reduced to a mere *activism*. True active participation does not mean to do something, but rather refers to a state of being that is fully aware of the liturgy's essence and sacredness.

Nowadays, the topics of *ad orientem*, Latin, and other aspects of Vatican II's reforms continue to be points of contention, but only due to misunderstanding the historical, sacramental, and theological teachings of the council. Among the most important steps to reclaiming Vatican II is restoring the proper understanding of the sacred liturgy as well as ensuring that the beauty of the Church's history, especially her artistic and architectural tradition, is reintegrated into the common life of the faithful.

Chapter Outline

I. *Sacrosanctum Concilium* (SC)

    A. First document to be promulgated and easily passed with super majority of bishops

    i.   Least controversial of the four major constitutions among the conciliar fathers, yet the most controversial of our time

        1. The sacred liturgy is described by *SC* as the primary and fundamental act of the Church (*SC* 10–11)

           a. *SC* is not so much a technical or rubrical text as a theological text

               i. The specific reforms are named *after* the spiritual reflections on the nature of the liturgy revealing the purpose of the council's reforms

B. The origin and nature of the liturgy according to Vatican II

    i.   The liturgy is not simply one function among many in the life of the Church, but rather the central and primary responsibility of Catholicism. All other acts of the Church flow from and are gauged by the liturgy (*SC* 10–11).

        1. What is the liturgy?

    ii. Liturgy distinguished into two aspects by Vatican II (*SC* 5–7)

        1. Ministry of reconciliation

           a. The Adamic cult versus the Christic cult

               i. St. Paul: 2 Cor 5:18

        2. Ministry of adoration

           a. Gen 2:15: *Abad* "cult" or "worship"

           b. The liturgy is the newly established and redeemed *abad* of the Father via the adoration of Christ

C. Active participation: The basic principle of reform

    i. Conciliar fathers recognized a need for the laity, religious, and clergy to better understand the essential nature of the sacraments, especially the Eucharist

       1. The phrase "active participation" becomes the guiding principle of this need for a renewed consciousness of the liturgical mystery

          a. Often misrepresented as *activism*

             i. True definition of "activity," also known as *actio*

            ii. Does *not* mean to "do more stuff," but rather to readily engage the reality with our whole person through contemplation, knowledge, and prayer

D. *Ad orientem* or *versus populum*

    i. Sadly, one of the most controversial issues in the so-called "liturgy wars"

       1. False dichotomy that is over-politicized by both paracouncil and traditionalism

          a. Note that both postures are utilized in different celebrations of both rites (that is, the closing prayer of Eucharistic Adoration, Benediction, Missal of St. Pius V, *dominus vobiscum*, and so on)

    ii. Scriptural and theological foundations of *ad orientem*

       1. Fundamental expression of Judeo-Christian liturgical prayer and private piety

          a. Supported by apostolic and patristic tradition

          b. Four major sources

             i. *Historical continuity with Judaism*

            ii. *Reveals our orientation to the New Temple, who is Jesus Christ*

          iii. *Unity with creation, that is, the restoration of communion with Creator*

          iv. *Eschatological nature of the Church as a "pilgrim people"*

    2. Where did the confusion come from and why?

    3. Pastoral ways to educate and popularize *ad orientem*

E. Latin and the vernacular

F. Other important reforms

    i. Three-year lectionary cycle

    ii. RCIA program

    iii. Preaching

G. The Divine Office: A forgotten treasure

    i. Transformative and untapped grace for the laity and parishes

        1. Among the most ancient practices of the Church and most accessible means to foster contemplation in parish communities

        2. Vatican II intends the Divine Office to be prayed not only by the clergy, but hopes the laity and especially families will likewise integrate it into their daily lives

H. Restoring beauty: Sacred music and church architecture

    i. The Church possesses one of the longest-standing artistic traditions in world history

        1. There is a desperate need to rehabilitate traditional art forms into the lives of our parishioners through church architecture and sacred music

Study Questions

1. Discuss the role of the liturgy in the life of the Church according to *SC* (par. 10–11).

2. Why is Christ called "The New Adam"?

3. Explain what active participation is and what it is not.

4. What is the role of silence in fostering active participation?

5. Explain the historical, scriptural, and theological origins of *ad orientem*.

6. Did Vatican II suppress the use of Latin in the sacred liturgy? Explain and give evidence from the document for your answer.

7. Name some other important reforms from *SC*.

8. What is the role of beauty in the liturgy? How can we promote beauty in our local parish communities?

Key Terms

Sacrosanctum Concilium (p. 39)

Liturgy as reconciliation (pp. 45–49)

Liturgy as adoration (pp. 50–53)

Active participation (p. 53–57)

Ad orientem and *versus populum* (pp. 61–68)

RCIA (pp. 77–78)

Divine Office (pp. 79–83)

CHAPTER 4

THE CHURCH

Chapter Summary

The Second Vatican Council is often referred to as the "Council of the Church." *Lumen Gentium* is the "hinge" document of the council as it represents nearly two hundred years of development in the field of ecclesiology, the theological discipline that studies the nature and origins of the Church. Due to the discovery of numerous patristic texts, ecclesiology experienced a revival during the nineteenth and twentieth centuries.

Vatican II describes the Church as the sacrament of salvation (*LG* 48). In other words, the Church is a *sacrament*. She is a visible sign of an invisible reality, namely, the salvation of Christ realized in history. The Catholic Church, therefore, is not an accident or coincidence; rather, Catholicism is God's will realized in the world. The Church is the way by which Christ continues to adore the Father and dwell in our midst. As the sacrament of salvation, the Catholic Church is also the sole Church of Christ: The fullness of faith "constituted and organized in the world as a society, subsists in the Catholic Church, which is governed by the successor of Peter and by the Bishops in communion with him" (*LG* 8). The paracouncil downplayed this teaching of Vatican II, thinking it too exclusive and sought to soften the distinctions between Catholicism and other religions, but, the council is clear in stating that the Catholic Church is the one true faith willed by Christ.

However, this should not lead to any sense of isolationism or triumphalism among Catholics. On the contrary. We are responsible for opening avenues of dialogue with our brothers and sisters from other Christian denominations as well as those who practice different religions entirely. The council dedicates significant energies to ensure that the Church remains evangelical in its attempts to both reconcile with Protestantism and Eastern Orthodoxy (also known as ecumenism) as well as interreligious dialogue.

Another crucial component of *LG* is its emphasis on the universal call to holiness and the People of God. Everyone is called to become a saint from the moment of their Baptism until their final breath. This is a vocation given to all Christians without discrimination. The Church is entrusted with fostering this call through a mutual cooperation among the clergy, religious and laity. Specifically, the laity are invited to realize their unique vocation in the Church as those who are called to be in the world but not of the world as they seek to witness to Christ in their daily lives.

There was a major debate during the council as to the role of the Blessed Virgin Mary in salvation history as well as her role in the life of the Church. Some bishops believed there should be a separate document dedicated to the Blessed Mother exclusively, while others asserted that she should be included in *LG*. Ultimately, the council decided to include Our Lady in the final chapter of *LG*, a very significant theological decision that sent a strong message about the relationship between Mary and the Church. For she is not simply an illustrious member of Catholicism. In fact, the Blessed Mother is the embodiment of Catholicism; she is the Church in person and as person. When you look at Mary, you see the Church. She simultaneously reveals what the Church is, that is, an adorer of Jesus Christ, while also being an example for all other members of the Church to follow. In this sense, Mary is the mother and model of the Church.

Chapter Outline

I. *Lumen Gentium* (*LG*)

  A. Considered the "hinge" or "defining" document of Vatican II

    i. Reveals the theological developments of *ressourcement* in two major ways

      1. Ecclesiology, also known as the study of the Church

      2. Mariology, also known as the study of the Blessed Virgin Mary

  B. The Church as the sacrament of salvation (*LG* 48)

    i. Vatican II describes the Church as the "sacrament of salvation"

      1. The Church is the sacrament of God's presence in the world. More specifically, it is the sacrament and sign of the Trinity, who has revealed himself in history as the Father, Son, and Holy Spirit (pp. 96–98)

        a. This revelation is manifested through the sacramental life, hierarchy (clergy), religious, and laity in complementarity with one another, also known as the "Body of Christ" (1 Cor 12)

        b. We encounter the living God through His Church and her mission

  C. The sole Church of Christ

    i. The uniqueness of Catholicism and ecumenism

      1. The Catholic Church is not a sacrament of the world, but the sacrament of salvation as she reminds the world of its vocation to recognize the kingship of Jesus Christ

        a. The paracouncil construed this notion seeing it as too exclusive or confrontational, often softening the lines of distinction between Catholicism and other Christian denominations or religions

 2. True ecumenism according to Vatican II

  a. Ecumenism versus interreligious dialogue

   i. Ecumenism pertains to dialogue between different Christian denominations

   ii. Interreligious dialogue pertains to the cooperation between different religions

  b. Four guiding principles of ecumenism

   i. Objective evaluation of differing theologies without prejudice or bias

   ii. Discourse between competent experts within the different faith communities about specific theological or scriptural issues

   iii. Cooperation between denominations on promoting the common good, social justice and areas of agreement

   iv. Examination of our faithfulness to Christ and his desire for unity among all Christians

 3. The Catholic Church's stance toward other Christians and other religions (*LG* 14–16)

  a. Controversial paragraph regarding the uniqueness of the Catholic Church as well as the Church's attitude toward other religions/faith traditions

   i. Often misrepresented by traditionalists as universalism

    1. In fact, Vatican II's teaching builds on patristic and Thomistic principles that recognize the "seeds of faith" in all

people that need to be brought to the fullness of truth

    ii. Does *not* dampen our evangelical responsibility. We preach the Gospel not only to save souls but also to bring all people to the joy of knowing Jesus Christ

D. The People of God and the universal call to holiness

    i. The Church is the New Israel revealed in both her hierarchy and members

    ii. Laity and holiness

        1. Vatican II is the first council in Church history to dedicate a significant section of a magisterial document on the laity

        2. Building on momentum present in the late nineteenth and early twentieth century, Vatican II highlights the fact that Baptism is a vocation in and of itself, that is, all people are called to become saints

           a. This also denotes the "priesthood of the faithful" as it reminds us that each Christian is baptized into a ministry of personal sanctification by which they witness to the truth of Christ

E. The Blessed Virgin Mary

    i. Vatican II featured a major debate about the Blessed Virgin Mary and how to address her role in the Church and salvation history

        1. Council fathers agree that Mary should not have her own document, but be included on the document on the Church

           a. Very important theological and pastoral decision as it highlights for the People of God the fact that Mary is not only a prestigious member of the Church, but the embodiment of the New Israel and Catholicism per se

   i. Mary's vocation is integral to the mission of Christ, not only as his mother, but also as his first disciple whose faith and fiat become the foundations of all Christian faith

   ii. There is no Christianity without Mary's active participation in salvation history

   iii. Mary is the Church in person and as person

Study Questions

1. Why is *Lumen Gentium (LG)* considered the "hinge" document of Vatican II?

2. What are the two major fields of theological study that contribute to the teachings of *LG*?

3. What does Vatican II mean by defining the Church as the "sacrament of salvation"? How does the Church witness to salvation in the world?

4. What is the council's teaching on ecumenism? On interreligious dialogue? Does the council teach universalism?

5. What is the "universal call to holiness"?

6. Briefly share what you learned about the role of Mary in salvation history.

Key Terms

Lumen Gentium (p. 93)

Johann Adam Möhler (p. 93)

St. John Henry Newman (p. 94)

CHAPTER 5

DIVINE REVELATION

Chapter Summary

Dei Verbum, is the shortest of the four major council documents. The topic of divine revelation was initially introduced in 1870 during the First Vatican Council, but not fully discussed because the council was shortened due to the Franco-Prussian War. Thus, there needed to be a deeper reflection on the essence and sources of divine revelation. Divine revelation was a topic of debate during the council and one of the more divisive subjects among the bishops.

At question was the relationship between tradition and sacred scripture, as well as the historicity and inerrancy of the Bible. Also, because of advances in biblical scholarship throughout the nineteenth and twentieth centuries there were a number of techniques and new methods of study that needed to be approved by the magisterium. In particular, use of the historical-critical method in Catholic scholarship was examined.

The document begins with a reflection on divine revelation, not only as the sacred scripture, but most importantly as Jesus Christ himself. The Word of God is not a book, but a Person. That Person has given himself to us in two ways, through sacred tradition (that is, liturgy, sacraments, and the magisterium) as well as sacred scripture (that is, the Bible). This is called the deposit of faith.

Tradition comes from the Latin *traditio*, meaning "to hand over." Jesus founded an infrastructure through which his presence could be mediated. The divine revelation of Christ entrusted to the apostles in the sacraments and preaching is preserved in sacred tradition.

Sacred scripture is the Holy Spirit's testament to the Word-made-flesh. When we reflect on the scriptures, we grow in our understanding and appreciation of Christ's life as well as how he is the fulfillment of all history. Vatican II reminds all Catholics of the responsibility to know and love the sacred scriptures. Thus, the council exhorts the faithful to an increased study of the Bible.

In the end, *DV* reminds us that we do not follow Christ secondhand. In order to follow him, we have to meet him and know him. Through both sacred tradition and sacred scripture as mediated by the magisterium, we encounter the living God and enter into a dynamic relationship with him.

Chapter Outline

I. *Dei Verbum (DV)*

    A. Shortest of the Vatican II major constitutions

        i. Like *Lumen Gentium*, it synthesizes the numerous developments in scholarship and theology of the *Ressourcement* movement

        ii. Discusses divine revelation as a deposit of faith composed of two sources, which are essentially cooperative

           1. Sacred tradition

           2. Sacred scripture

    B. What is divine revelation?

        i. The "Word of God" is not a something but a *someone*, namely Jesus Christ, the Word-made-flesh (Jn 1:14)

1. Sacred scripture and sacred tradition are the ways that Christ actively relates and reveals himself to us through the Church

C. Sacred tradition and sacred scripture

   i. Neither of these sources are superior to the other. Both represent a two-fold way by which God reveals himself to humanity

     1. Intended to be complimentary

       a. Sacred tradition is represented by the magisterium and transmitted through sacraments and preaching (p. 132)

       b. Sacred scripture (also known as the Bible) is the Holy Spirit's testament to the Word-made-flesh

D. Interpreting sacred scripture

   i. Multiple developments in the field of biblical theology since the sixteenth century, especially in the realm of archeology, literary criticism, and exegesis (that is, the historical-critical method)

     1. The popes of the nineteenth and twentieth centuries began to integrate this newfound knowledge into biblical scholarship, especially Pius X and Pius XII

     2. Vatican II encourages biblical theologians to make use of the modern tools and resources so as to enrich the Church's appreciation of scripture as well as better preach to the People of God

       a. The council also reiterates the importance of laity studying the scriptures as well as the Church Fathers (that is, patristics)

Study Questions

1. What is divine revelation?

2. What is the "deposit of faith"?

3. In your own words, define sacred tradition.

4. In your own words, define sacred scripture.

5. What were some of the developments that took place in the centuries preceding Vatican II that led to an emphasis on sacred scripture at the council?

6. What are some ways you can enrich your parish's appreciation of sacred tradition and sacred scripture?

Key Terms

Dei Verbum (p. 127)

Divine revelation (pp. 128–131)

Sacred tradition (pp. 131–134)

Sacred scripture (pp. 134–139)

Historical-critical method (pp. 134–137)

CHAPTER 6

THE CHURCH AND THE MODERN WORLD

Chapter Summary

Gaudium et Spes is the last of the four major documents of Vatican II. As we noted in chapter 2, there is a fundamental logic to the council. The life of the Church is sourced in the sacred liturgy. It is from the work of the liturgy that the Church's essential nature shines forth. This Church is nourished and guided by divine revelation, as given to us in sacred scripture and sacred tradition. In *GS*, the council focuses on the natural consequence of the liturgy and divine revelation: evangelization.

GS stands apart from the other major council documents as a *pastoral* constitution rather than a *dogmatic* constitution. Overall, it represents a true shift in the Church's posture toward the world. The primary concern is not a particular doctrine of the Church, but the care of souls. It guides the Church in her mission of evangelization and salvation. *GS* is the longest of the four major council documents and discusses a wide variety of topics, especially in the areas of social justice and missionary activity. Likewise, there is a whole section dedicated to the Sacrament of Marriage and the role of the family in culture.

The most impressive thing about *GS* is its ability to "judge the signs of the times" (Mt 16:3). The document begins with a basic question: What is the situation of humanity in the world today? The council answers, "Man is growing in awareness that the forces he has unleashed are in his own hands and that it is up to him to control them or be enslaved by them. Here lies the modern dilemma" (*GS* 9). The rest of the constitution attempts to address the origins and solutions to this observation noting the increasingly secular culture of the West and the dangers of becoming an overly empirical or socio-economic society void of religious sentiment. Paragraph 22 is the central statement of *GS* as it asserts the centrality of Christ in civilization and the role of the Church to reveal the truth of Christ to the world.

No council in history dedicated more effort to the laity than Vatican II. In addition to expounding on the lay state of life, the council fathers also provide a powerful reflection on the vocation of marriage as a sacrament and its foundational role in establishing and maintaining a healthy society. When reading the council's teachings on marriage and the family, we are reminded that the only true way we can heal culture is by upholding the dignity of human sexuality and God's will for creation through the family.

Chapter Outline

I. *Gaudium et Spes* (*GS*)

   A. Unique among the four major documents as it is labeled a *pastoral* constitution, not a dogmatic constitution

      i. Reflects on the role of the Church in the modern world and her mission to evangelize

         1. Heavily influenced by Karol Wojtyla, also known as St. John Paul II

      ii. *GS* has a tone of openness that is quite different from previous Councils. Instead of being composed as a series of rejections or condemnations about society, it seeks to identify what is best in culture while also noting the dangers of secularism

B. Some major themes in *GS*

    i. The state of the modern world

    ii. Threats to culture (atheism, agnosticism, secularism, socialism, communism, materialism, and so on)

       1. Dignity of the human person

    iii. Mission of the Church and the need for faith

    iv. Marriage and the family

    v. The proper development of culture and evangelization

C. Jesus Christ: The center of civilization

    i. Dichotomy between pre-modern and post-modern view of the world

       1. Pre-modern: The world is created by a loving God who has given it to us as a gift and responsibility

       2. Post-modern: The world is pure matter created by a series of random scientific events with no ultimate purpose or destiny. It can be utilized according to the wants and needs of humanity

    ii. Paragraph 22 of *GS* is considered the defining section of *GS* as it asserts that Jesus Christ is the center of all creation and the revelation of humanity's ultimate goal

       1. Only when Christ is at the center of civilization can we acquire a healthy and complete view of the world and society

D. Preservation of a humane culture and social justice

    i. *GS* best known for its emphasis on the Church's role in culture and social justice

1. The Church is called to advocate on behalf of the weak and disenfranchised no matter what their background or status

2. The Church must work with governments and political structures to ensure the dignity of the human person is preserved

E. Vatican II on marriage and the family

   i. The Second Vatican Council dedicates a significant portion of *GS* to marriage and the family, recognizing the many struggles of society and that they are rooted in a breakdown of the family unit

      1. In particular, Vatican II realizes the threats against the family through "hedonism" and "contraception"

         a. These warnings are increasingly relevant in light of the current trends in culture, especially on the topic of human sexuality as the LGBTQ agenda is regularly promoted in the entertainment industry, the scourge of pornography is traumatizing more and more of our youth, and abortion is available throughout the world on demand

      2. The council is clear that the *only* way we can truly heal and restore culture is by healing and restoring the family

         a. The priesthood is integral to this process as clergy are called to cooperate with parents in their vocation to raise children in the faith

      3. This begins with adequate marriage preparation

         a. Two steps

            i. Christian education

     1. Marriage preparation begins long before someone is engaged. The first school of marriage is the family and the parish where the child receives both their personal and catechetical formation. Mentored by their faith community, they learn the true meaning of love

  ii. Marriage preparation in parishes

     1. Likewise, marriage-preparation programs are in desperate need for a renewed attention worthy of a sacrament. As Millennials and Gen Z start getting engaged, they will need a special guidance due to the moral decline of their culture and a general lack of interpersonal and sexual education

Study Questions

1. What distinguishes *Gaudium et Spes (GS)* from the other three major constitutions? Who was the well-known theologian and saint that greatly influenced the style and tone of *GS*?

2. Name three major themes of *GS*.

3. What is considered the defining or hinge paragraph of *GS* and what does it assert?

4. Vatican II is unique in regard to its emphasis on marriage and the family. Briefly explain what the council teaches about the role of marriage and the family in healing culture. What can your parish do to enrich its marriage formation program as well as educate the youth of the community on the dignity of human sexuality and marriage?

Key Terms

Gaudium et Spes (p. 141)

Karol Wojtyla (pp. 141–142)

Pastoral constitution (p. 141)

Gaudium et Spes, par. 22 (p. 147)

Marriage and the family (pp. 151–159)

Marriage preparation (p. 160)

CHAPTER 7

WHAT NOW?

Chapter Summary

The Second Vatican Council is among the most important events in the Church's history, yet many people remain unfamiliar with its teachings and its vision continues to be widely misrepresented by both critics and proponents. We live at a pivotal moment in Church history. Our generation has been entrusted by the Holy Spirit with the proper implementation of Vatican II. This requires us to both know and treasure the teachings of the council. In *Reclaiming Vatican II*, Fr. Blake reviews the post-conciliar period and unmasks the narratives of the paracouncil. Likewise, he asserts the need to read the documents first-hand and return to the true intention of Vatican II. With that in mind, Fr. Blake offers several ways forward, building on the legacy of the United States' first bishop, John Carroll.

Carroll knew that the answer to securing Catholic faith in America depended on two things: *piety* and *education*. The sacred liturgy is always the basis of true reform. It is the premier activity of the Church and the source of her holiness. Reclaiming the Church's liturgy from the paracouncil is step one. And this begins with the sacraments and the intentional restoration of beauty in accord with tradition. It starts with the priest who is the shepherd of his community. Wherever the shepherd leads, the sheep will follow. If we want to reclaim Vatican II in its fullness, it will require the cooperation and example of the clergy. To this end, the *ars celebrandi* will prove indispensable, as priests embody the true spirit of Vatican II in their liturgical and pastoral activity. This demands that the priest be a man of prayer and devotion, especially for the Eucharist. The Mass must be the center of his universe. Everything else that takes place in the parish flows from the Mass.

In addition to the *ars celebrandi*, the gradual reintegration of certain traditions will prove vital. This is especially important in the realm of sacred music, sacred art, sacred vessels, and architecture. Furthermore, the education and catechesis of the faithful is essential. Teaching the People of God about the traditions, theologies, and humanities of the Catholic Church is a vital pastoral responsibility. Hosting classes for furthering faith formation, even for those who are fully initiated into the Church, is a great source of renewal.

We find ourselves at a crucial moment in Church history. It is not an accident that you are alive here and now. We do not have to waste time trying to figure out our task. The Holy Spirit gave it to us plainly in the Second Vatican Council. All we need to do now is reclaim it.

Chapter Outline

I. A review of what we have learned

    A. In *Reclaiming Vatican II*, we learned about the undue influence of the paracouncil throughout the past sixty years and how it has negatively affected the implementation and reception of Vatican II

        i. Thus, there is a need to rediscover the true spirit of the council freed from polemics and faithful to the text as written

II. Reclaiming Vatican II

    A. Lessons from Bishop John Carroll

    i.   First bishop of the United States, installed August 15, 1790

   ii.   The Church in the United States was plagued by a lack of catechesis among the faithful and a disorganized presbyterate

  iii.   Bishop Carroll highlighted two priorities for his episcopate and its mission to renew and organize the nascent faith in the United States

       1. Piety

       2. Education

  iv.   Piety

       1. Carroll's pastoral letters to his clergy emphasize the need to restore liturgical and sacramental devotion among the faithful

          a. This is primarily accomplished through a renewed focus on the sanctity of the Eucharist and frequent confession

          b. Carroll realized there could be no development of the faith without the solemnity and beauty of the liturgy

          c. The surest way to inspire piety among the faithful is through the holiness of their clergy

       2. *Ars celebrandi*: It starts with the priest

          a. The fastest way to effect positive change in a community is through the piety of priests

              i. The health of a parish community is dependent on the holiness of its shepherds

             ii. The demeanor, attitude, and devotion that a priest has toward their sacramental ministry is known as the *ars celebrandi* or the "art of the celebrant/celebration"

3. Do not underestimate the power of small, intentional steps

   a. In our society, there is a temptation to want immediate results, but that is not the case when it comes to reform in the Church

      i. At least three to five years to establish long-lasting changes

      ii. Takes place in two stages

      iii. Years 1–3: "The Catechetical Stage"

         1. These first years should be dedicated to building a pastoral relationship with parishioners as well as dedicating resources (financial or otherwise) to faith formation for the whole community
            a. Monthly classes on Church history, the liturgy, patristics, scripture study, and so on

         2. These are also the years when the infrastructures to sustain the "implementation stage" are put into place

      iv. Years 3–5: "The Implementation Stage"

         1. These final years are dedicated to implementing the teachings, ideas, and long-term goals for the parish
            a. Now that the faithful have been educated and informed about the pastoral vision for their parish, they will hopefully be more keen to receive any necessary changes and embrace them as their own

4. Be committed to teaching and learning—and evangelizing

     a. Educating the priests and staff of our parishes is essential

        i. In many ways, the parish culture is based on the overall culture that exists among the priests and their staff/pastoral team

        ii. If the priests and staff are excited about the Church and its teachings, then that will naturally spillover into the rest of the parish

           1. Having a faith-filled, joyful, and well-educated parish team is one of the most important elements of a successful parish and will prove vital to the proper implementation of Vatican II

           2. Parish staff should be well-studied in the documents of Vatican II and each office (faith formation, administration, marriage preparation, music direction, and so on) should be asking how they are integrating the documents of the council into their daily work

     b. In all things, the joy of the Gospel is our shared focus as we seek to reclaim Vatican II for this generation of the Church

Study Questions

1. Summarize the main thesis of *Reclaiming Vatican II* as presented in the beginning of chapter 7.

2. Who was Bishop John Carroll and what two things can we learn from his pastoral vision for the Church in the United States?

3. What roles do piety and education have to play in our own time? How can they be implemented into your local parish?

4. What is the *ars celebrandi*?

5. Identify and explain the two stages of implantation for a parish Fr. Blake discusses in his five-year plan.

6. What are some ways you can integrate the teachings and instructions of the four major documents of Vatican II into your personal ministry at the parish?

Key Terms

John Carroll (p. 165)

Ars celebrandi (pp. 166–168)

Fr. Blake Britton is a priest and theologian from the Diocese of Orlando. His writings are featured in multiple anthologies and publications including *Evangelization & Culture Journal*, *The National Catholic Register*, *Ignatius Press* and *Ave Maria Press*. He is also the author of *Reclaiming Vatican II: What It (Really) Said, What It Means, and How It Calls Us to Renew the Church*.

Britton has been featured on EWTN, cohosts the landmark YouTube series *God and Gaming* and regularly appears on other media outlets. He is cohost, with Brandon Vogt, of *The Burrowshire Podcast* focusing on millennial evangelization and theology.

AVE

AVE MARIA PRESS

Founded in 1865, Ave Maria Press,
a ministry of the Congregation of
Holy Cross, is a Catholic publishing
company that serves the spiritual and
formative needs of the Church and its
schools, institutions, and ministers;
Christian individuals and families; and
others seeking spiritual nourishment.

For a complete listing of titles from

Ave Maria Press

Sorin Books

Forest of Peace

Christian Classics

visit www.avemariapress.com

AVE MARIA PRESS
Notre Dame, IN
A Ministry of the United States Province of Holy Cross